To: Jo,

Happy 80th Birthday

Love and best wishes

From: Pat

23rd July 2009.

PORTRAIT OF EXETER

PORTRAIT OF
EXETER

LEE PENGELLY

HALSGROVE

First published in Great Britain in 2007

Title Page: **City of Exeter Coat of Arms**
Coat of arms detail on a quayside building. The inscription 'Semper Fidelis': Ever Faithful.

British Library Cataloguing-in-Publication Data
A CIP record for this title is available from the British Library

ISBN 978 1 84114 605 8

HALSGROVE
Halsgrove House
Ryelands Industrial Estate
Bagley Road, Wellington
Somerset TA21 9PZ
T: 01823 653777
F: 01823 216796
email: sales@halsgrove.com
website: www.halsgrove.com

Printed and bound by D'Auria Industrie Grafiche Spa, Italy

FOREWORD

by Philip Bostock – Chief Executive of Exeter City Council

As a City with over 2000 years of history, Exeter presents a whole variety of images to the visitor. The Romans determined its basic form – the lowest crossing point of the Exe was where the Roman army chose to establish a Legionary Fortress, on a site that could be easily defended. The Roman citizens later built a defensive wall – much improved subsequently, particularly during the Civil War – and today's linear route from the river up Fore Street, through the High Street and on to Sidwell Street broadly follows the basic form of Roman Exeter's development.

During the intervening two millennia, the City's changing role is marked by a range of buildings and structures. The Norman gatehouse to Exeter Castle is a powerful symbol of William the Conqueror's imprint on the South West, dating from 1068. St Peter's Cathedral is the jewel in Exeter's crown, built between c.1112 and 1370. The Exeter Ship Canal – Britain's first pound lock canal – was completed in 1566 and since has been extended and deepened. The City's Grade I Listed Custom House was built in 1681 at the height of Exeter's prosperity as a port, and that and the Quay remain as beautiful reminders of the City's commercial past.

Fast forward to the present and Exeter now displays a very different commercial base, but still with the same cultural and historic heart. The Met Office's world headquarters on the edge of the City underlines Exeter's growing reputation for science and for knowledge-based industries. It works collaboratively with the University of Exeter – itself a rapidly expanding top 20 university. Although the City has only 120 000 residents, its employment base is considerably larger with 86 000 jobs based in Exeter. It is an economy which is amongst the fastest growing in the country.

The regeneration of Exeter is rapid, in particular, with the completion in 2007 of the rejuvenated Princesshay – a retail-led regeneration scheme with substantial housing, tourist facilities and a stunning 'public realm'. It all combines to make Exeter truly the 'Regional Capital'.

I hope you enjoy this introduction to Exeter and moreover that you are tempted to visit its many and varied attractions.

Exeter Cathedral
The Cathedral has been at the heart of the city for almost a thousand years. Building began in the twelfth century,
fifty years or so after the Norman invasion.

INTRODUCTION

This book presented me with the challenge to produce a visual record of the City of Exeter and outlying areas. I was aware that it would have to include well-known views and buildings, old and new. I have tried to include as many as possible and I hope that I have done the City justice with this book.

A small percentage of images from my back catalogue are included in this book, however because my photographic style is constantly changing I wanted to add my own personal stamp on this book with new work, and this commission gave me a great opportunity to do this. I have included the familiar and not so familiar and tried throughout to do this with aesthetically pleasing images. Exeter is an evolving city with the modern and historic side by side. As a photographer this diversity is irresistible; I have enjoyed the whole process of producing this book immensely and hope that you too will enjoy the book for many years to come.

Behind the Lens – Three main elements go toward my photography – light, composition and timing. These form the basis for each picture I produce. I love the warm light of dawn and dusk and try to photograph at these times. During the Spring and early Summer this meant getting up at 4am for a dawn vigil on the banks of the Exeter canal. The atmosphere and light at these times is magical and worth the early start.

My equipment has changed time and again over the years but this book marks my commitment to the digital medium. Love it or hate it digital is here to stay and I have embraced its versatility, control and overall quality. For this book I have used the Nikon D2x, and Fuji S2pro cameras along with lenses ranging from 10mm–300mm. I would be lost without my trusty Manfrotto tripod, a pain to carry but essential for those low-light moments. I am not into heavy manipulation of images and only use the bare minimum of exposure controls in Photoshop, preferring to get the image right in the field with physical filters such as ND graduates, polarisers and warm-ups.

ACKNOWLEDGEMENTS

I would like to thank the following for their invaluable help in the preparation of this book.

Philip Bostock, Chief Executive of Exeter City Council.

Staff at the Tourist Information Centre, Exeter City Centre.

David at Exeter Memories, www.exetermemories.co.uk.

Red Coat city guides, Exeter City Centre.

Spectrum Photo Labs, Plymouth.

Jan Barwick, *Devon Life.*

Miller's Crossing Bridge
A giant millstone lies at the end of the
modern pedestrian bridge near Exbridges.

Left
The Imperial
The prominent semi-circular conservatory
was added later to this late-Georgian
building, now a popular pub.

Miller's Crossing
An early morning jogger runs
across Miller's Crossing pedestrian
bridge over the River Exe.

Southernhay West

Barnfield Theatre
The theatre was opened in 1891
as Barnfield Hall and paid for largely
by the philanthropy of George Franklin.
The panelling on the exterior of the
building is decorated with theatrical
scenes and characters.

Right
Southernhay
The beautiful Georgian terraced houses
are now used as commercial offices
by architects, solicitors, banks and a
variety of other companies.

Queen Street Detail
Stone carving overlooking Queen Street, next to the Royal Albert Memorial Museum.

Left
Royal Albert Memorial Museum
This fine Victorian building was completed in 1866,
and the museum and art gallery are favourite places to visit
for tourists and residents alike.

Exeter Cathedral, Evening
At dusk the street lamps go on and
add atmosphere to the Cathedral Close.

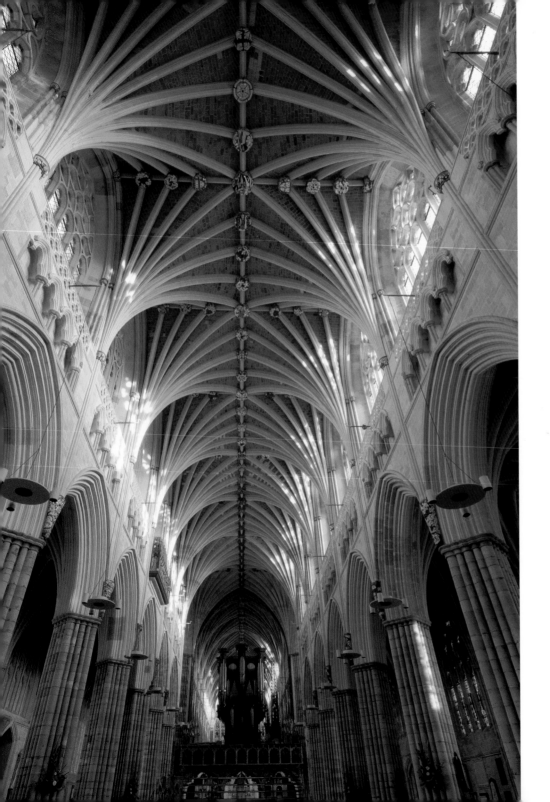

Cathedral Stone Carving
The façade of Exeter Cathedral is highly decorated with carvings such as these.

Left
Exeter Cathedral
The beautiful detailing inside the Cathedral takes your breath away. Sit here on a quiet day and take in the architectural brilliance.

Cathedral Angel
A delicately carved stone angel on
the façade of Exeter Cathedral.

Right
Exeter Cathedral
Low evening sunlight bleeds
through the Cathedral windows,
lighting the stonework details.

Mol's Coffee House
Said to have been opened by an Italian
of that name in the sixteenth century,
legend has it that the great Sea Captains
Drake, Raleigh and Hawkins met here
to discuss their triumphs.

Left
Cathedral Close Street Café
Al fresco coffee in a street café, with the
backdrop of Exeter's famous Cathedral.

The Royal Clarence Hotel, Cathedral Close
The hotel (left) also houses the restaurant of Michelin Star chef Michael Caine.

Cathedral Guardian
A stone carving overlooking Exeter
Cathedral's grounds.

Cathedral Close
Such beautiful Georgian architecture is seen everywhere in Exeter;
shops, houses, all beautifully maintained.

Right
Richard Hooker Statue
Born in 1554 in Heavitree, Exeter, Renaissance preacher and author, Hooker studied
at Corpus Christi college in Oxford, taking Holy orders in 1581.

Queen Street Clock Tower
This ornate clock tower was erected in
1897 by Mrs Louisa A. Miles in memory
of her husband who died in 1881 aged 91.
He was an Exeter magistrate
and philanthropist.

St David's Church on Queen's Terrace
The renowned Exeter physician Thomas Glass is buried in the church grounds.

Exeter St David's Station
Designed by Francis Fox in 1864, the building replaced the original I.K. Brunel station of 1844.

Exeter Central Station, Queen Street
Originally named Queen Street Station before it was burnt down
in June 1927. It was rebuilt with the present frontage in 1934.

The House That Moved
This medieval building was moved in
its entirety from nearby Edmund Street
in 1961 to make way for a new road.

Right
West Street
St Mary Steps Church with its famous
Matthew the Miller clock

Stepcote Hill lantern
Medieval details like this are everywhere in Exeter.

Stepcote Hill
Timber detail on a house.

Right
Stepcote Hill
One of the oldest streets in Exeter.
It was the main route into the city in
Roman times.

Old Exe Bridge
The ruins of the old Exe Bridge sit
beside the busy Exe Bridges roundabout,
a reminder of quieter times.

Right
City Wall
The city wall has not been
intact for many years but there
are still remnants such as this, at
Athelstan's Tower, which give an
idea of its scale.

Northernhay Gardens
Summer flowers and war memorial.

Left
War Memorial
The First World War memorial was
dedicated on 29 April 1923.
It cost at that time around
£6000 and is one of the finest
examples in the country.

Right
City Wall
A variety of summer flowers in the
shelter of the city wall.

Volunteer Force Memorial, Northenhay
The memorial statue of the Volunteer Force
in Northernhay gardens. The Volunteer Force
later became the Territorial Army.

Burnet Patch Bridge
Named after Mayor Burnet Patch this iron pedestrian bridge was placed here in 1814 between Southernhay and Cathedral Close. The city wall was cut and the bridge placed at the site of a thirteenth-century tower.

St Nicholas Priory
Only a quarter of the original priory
remains, half was destroyed at the
Dissolution in the sixteenth century, the
remainder is known as The Mint.

Oddfellows Hall
The Oddfellows Society was established in Exeter in 1845
to help working men of the city.

St Catherine's Chapel
In 1942 bombing destroyed the almhouses and chapel here. The council
landscaped the grounds around the remains as a memorial to that night.
The site now holds the striking 'Marking Time' glass sculptures.

'Marking Time'
Created by Patricia McKinnon-Day, the 'Marking Time' glass contains artefacts dating from Roman times up to the present day, including a Coke can!

War Memorial
In Northernhay Gardens overlooking Exeter College campus.

Left
Iron Bridge
In 1834 this bridge was built to ease entry into the city via North Street. It was manufactured
in sections at a foundry at Blaina ironworks in Wales, then shipped to Exeter
through the Exeter canal.

St Olave's Church, Fore Street
Founded as a palace chapel by Gytha, mother of King Harold who was killed in the battle of Hastings.
The medieval bell has the inscription 'Voce mew viva depello cuncta nociva',
'By my lively voice I disperse all that is harmful'.

Left
St Michael's, Mount Dinham
This is the highest spire West of Salisbury, measured at 70m (230ft).

Princesshay
Large sculptures at Princesshay offer a
varied range of uses to shoppers and
their children: a comfy seat and
climbing apparatus among them.

Right
Princesshay Apartments
New architecture sits alongside old;
a prime property location in the city
The new apartments were much sought
after, with buyers camping out in the
street on purchase day.

Princesshay Precinct
From design to reality, shoppers make the most of a nice day
at the new Princesshay shopping precinct.

Right
Eastgate, Princesshay
The modern architecture of the new Eastgate building rises over Paris Street.

Eastgate Building, Princesshay
Eastgate's elliptical glass-and-steel
building elegantly reflecting
the blue sky.

Riverside Leisure Centre
The modern city swimming pool now stands on the site previously occupied by
Austin car dealers P. Pike & Co Ltd, whose workshops in wartime were used to repair Spitfires.

Cathedral View
A fine view of the Cathedral,
is offered to the residents of
Princesshay's new apartments.

Sidwell Street Odeon Cinema
Exeter's oldest surviving cinema on Sidwell Street. The first film shown
here was *Charge of the Light Brigade* in 1937.

**Year of the Pedestrian Statue,
High Street**
By sculptor Carole Vincent and
placed in the High Street in 1989.

City Bank Pigeons, Cathedral Close
Pigeons nesting under the former City Bank signage.

Gandy Street
Unique shops, restaurants and boutiques give Gandy Street
it's character popular with locals and tourists alike.

Gandy Street
A wonderful mix of architectural styles in this quiet corner of Gandy Street.

Pinces Gardens, St Thomas
This wisteria tunnel stands on the site of William Lucombe's nursery founded in 1720.

Exeter Airport
The City's airport offers international flights to a number of foreign and domestic destinations,
and recent renovations have brought many benefits to those travelling.

Mute Swan
A female swan nesting in
reeds on the banks of the Exe.

Right
Exminster Marshes
New housing overlooking
marshland at Exminster.

Barbara Hepworth Statue, Exeter University
There are twenty-five sculptures in the grounds of Exeter University's
Streatham Campus, a unique setting in which to view works of art.

Vivian ap Rhys Pryce sculpture
A fascinating water sculpture
alongside the Peter Chalk centre on
Exeter University's Streatham campus.

River Creedy, Dawn
A misty dawn on the River Creedy.

Left
Cowley Bridge
Built originally in the coaching era
the bridge is now almost too narrow for
modern traffic. The busy A377
Crediton road runs through here
and a constant stream of traffic
uses the route on a daily basis.

River Mist
Dawn mist hangs over the River Creedy at Cowley bridge;
the river joins the main Exe river further downstream.

Right
River Exe, Topsham
The River Exe runs alongside Exminster marshes, a popular spot for birdwatching.

Topsham View
Topsham town viewed from the bank of Exeter canal at Exminster.

River Exe, Storm
A storm brews over the River Exe near Topsham.

Exeter Canal
Dawn light on Exeter canal.
Spring wildflowers grow abundantly
along the banks.

A Cycle Friendly City
A cyclist on his way
to work in Exeter.

Canal and City View
The towpath alongside Exeter's canal provides a great
cycle route for energetic, early morning cyclists.

Exeter Canal, Early Morning
Summer dawn over the canal near Salmonpool bridge,
a good spot to see kingfishers and herons.

Gabriel's Wharf
An old boat lies quietly alongside
Gabriel's Wharf.

Homes on the Canal, Gabriels Wharf
A row of modern homes reflected in the still water of Exeter canal. Location, location, location!

Left
Double Locks Pub
Built in 1701 as a lock-keepers cottage, it was rebuilt in 1820 by James Green when the canal basin was expanded. The building is now a popular waterside pub and hotel.

Distant Cathedral
The unmistakable towers of
Exeter Cathedral overlook the
canal at Gabriel's Wharf.

Turf Locks
Turf Locks canal, early morning

Trews Weir Suspension Bridge
Built in 1935 as a crossing for the workers at Willeys Foundry.

Early Jogger
Summer mornings jogging along the canal path with
your dogs, what better way to start the day.

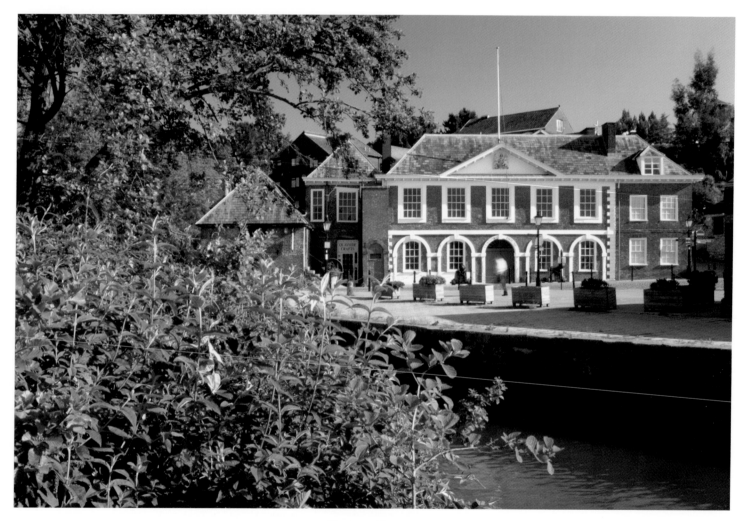

Custom House
Built in 1681 this stately building on
Exeter's quayside is full of maritime character.

Custom House
A huge cannon stands outside the Custom House on the Quay.

Cricklepit Bridge
Vibrantly coloured canoes
for hire on the River Exe.

Cricklepit Bridge
This striking pedestrian bridge spans the River Exe and provides
a thoroughfare to busy commuters on foot and on bikes.

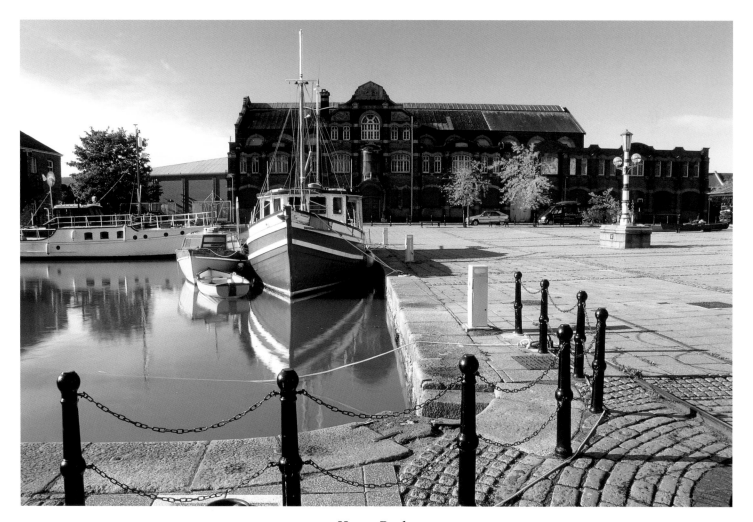

Haven Banks
The canal basin at Haven Banks.

Left
Butts Ferry
If you are too tired to walk the long way this little ferry will take
you across the Exe for a small fee. The first passenger ferry ran here around 1641.

Gabriel's Wharf

Turf Locks
The Turf Locks hotel isn't actually in Exeter but it is an important location, situated at the mouth of the Exeter canal.

The Port Royal Pub, near Haven Banks
In 1850 a freak whirlwind picked
up a four-oared gig and flung it in the air
as bemused onlookers sat by and watched.

Exe Estuary
The Exe estuary on a Summer morning.

Piazza Terracina, Haven Banks
Named in 1996 after Exeter's twinned Italian town the area is a great place to unwind and watch the world go by.

Exeter Quay, Arches
Various antique, craft and furniture stores line the quayside.

The Armillary, Exeter Quay
Roger Dean's bronze sculpture of
an armillary, an astronomical
instrument used by sailors.

No 44 Quay House
No 44 has Exeter's coat of arms
on it's Dutch gable façade.

Colleton Crescent
A fine Georgian crescent built by
Matthew Nosworthy. It featured in the TV series
the *Onedin Line,* and in a painting by J. M. W. Turner.

Fore Street, Topsham
Georgian building in Topsham's Fore Street.

Fore Street, Topsham
The narrow streets of Topsham are lined
with restaurants, galleries and interesting shops.

Topsham Church
Spring daffodils at Topsham church alongside the River Exe.

Left
Wixels, Topsham
This Dutch-gabled waterfront house takes it name from the building opposite,
the former site of 'Wigzells Spiral Fluted Nail Company'.

Phoenix Arts Centre, Gandy Street
Situated on the edge of the Norman
Motte of Rougemont Castle; a centre
for drama, arts and dance.

Left
Hotel Barcelona, Magdalen Street
The former West of England
Eye Infirmary, used briefly by
Exeter University before being
opened as a splendid hotel in 2001.

Rougemont Castle
People drinking coffee in the shade of a street café with the eleventh-century Norman gate tower in the background.

Exeter Catacombs
Built under the city walls to house coffins in vaults reached by a central passage.
The Egyptian styled façade and quiet location give the place an eerie feeling.
The Catacombs can be visited with a Red Coat guide.

Exeter School
The school on Victoria Park Road used to be the John the Baptist hospital buildings.

Well Park
Built in 1870 this old brewery narrowly missed destruction
in the Second World War when a German bomb bounced
down the road and exploded outside.

Jaguar Car Showrooms
This Matford car showroom is reminiscent of 1930's architectural style
but the cars on the forecourt couldn't be more up to date.

Left
The Picture House, Bartholomew Street
This striking modern cinema was opened in 1996, partly funded by the National Lottery Heritage Fund.

St James Park
The 'Grecians' red and white stadium
of Exeter City Football Club.

High Street at Christmas
The busy main High Street in Exeter.

Left
High Street at Christmas
The gateway to Princesshay
shopping centre on High Street. The
Exeter Riddle statue by Michael Fairfax
has verses from the tenth-century
Exeter Book inscribed on it.

Exeter Guildhall
The illuminated Guildhall overlooks the busy High Street.

Exeter Guildhall
This is the oldest civic building in the country.

Dingles
Sixties architecture viewed through the
stone window of St Catherine's chapel.

Three Gables, Cathedral Close
Dating from the seventeenth
century these buildings have cellars
lined with Heavitree stone.

Tudor Detailing
The ornate Tudor frontage of the
former J&G Ross premises.

Left
Tudor Houses, High Street
Only the frontage remains of these
Tudor houses, once the offices of the
Express & Echo and *Western Times*
newspapers.

Exeter Guildhall
The late evening sun makes the stonework of the Guildhall glow.

Wynards Hospital, Magdalen Street
These former almshouses were founded in the fifteenth century.
They have a history of alterations through the seventeenth, eighteenth,
nineteenth centuries, and even in modern times have been renovated.

143 Fore Street
Charles Dickens was a friend of
Thomas Latimer who was the
editor of the *Western Times*
based at No.143.

St Pancras Church, Guildhall Centre
One of the oldest Christian sites in England the church sits amongst
modern buildings in the centre of the Guildhall shopping precinct.

St Martin's Church, Cathedral close
One of the oldest churches in Exeter,
it was consecrated by Bishop Leofric
in 1065. An inscription of the Ten
Commandments is thought to have survived
under paintwork behind the altar.

Looking Forward, Bronze Sculpture
Sited in the Guildhall shopping centre this sculpture,
by Peter Thursby commemorates the Queen's Silver Jubilee.

Millennium Mosaic
Unveiled in 2000 this mosaic has 1000 blocks decorated to convey the theme 'A moment in time in Exeter'.

Queen Victoria Statue, Queen Street
Overlooking Queen Street this statue
is actually a copy of the original carved
in wood; it was re-cast in Fibreglass.

Left
The Deerstalker, Northernhay
The bronze Deerstalker statue at the
entrance of Northernhay gardens.

White Hart Inn, South Street
One of Exeter's most famous Inns.

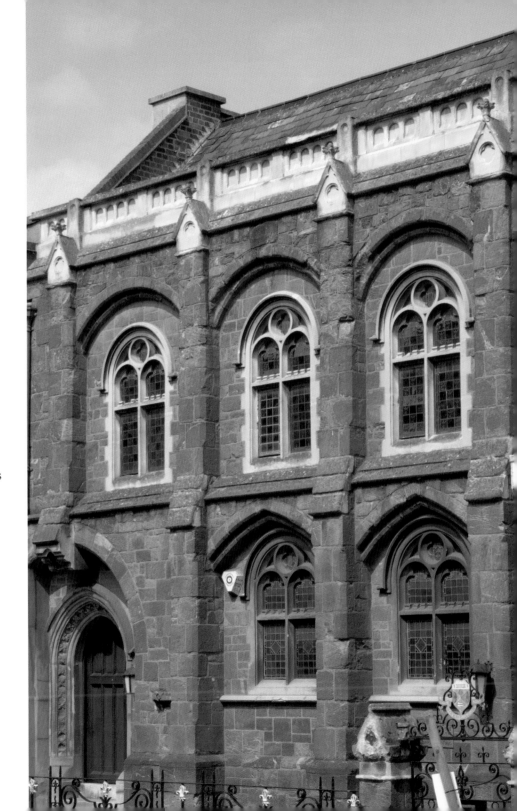

Tuckers Hall

Exeter was once a city employing hundreds
of weavers, tuckers and shearman in the
woollen industry. In 1470 they were given
a plot of land on which to build a chapel,
now known as Tuckers Hall.

The Mint Lane
This narrow lane leads down
to the Mint.

The Mint Church
This Catholic church stands on
the site of 21, The Mint.

St Thomas Parish Church
Built in local red sandstone the
church dates from 1657. Before the
First World War there were still
public stocks in the churchyard.

Ship Inn, Martins Lane
Exeter's maritime history is echoed in
this traditional pub sign showing a sixteenth-
century ship leaning to port on a rough sea.

Snayle Tower, Bartholomew Terrace
Once a thirteenth-century
lookout overlooking the Exe.

Bartholomew Terrace
Up to Saxon times this area was known as 'Little Britayne'.

Reed Hall, Exeter University
A beautiful Victorian Italianate house
surrounded by terraced gardens planted
with rare plants, flowers and trees.

Left
Northcott Theatre
This well-known theatre stands on the
Streatham campus at Exeter University.

Ide Ford Cottages
These quaint thatched cottages sit beside the ford in Ide. During Summer
the flowers turn this into a 'chocolate box' view.

Right
Sunflower Crop
These fields produce a different crop each season; sunflowers for the Summer.

Haldon Belvedere
Also known as Lawrence Castle this prominent white edifice, on the Haldon Hills
overlooking Exeter, can be seen from miles around.

Alphington Church
St Michaels and All Angels church in
Alphington, built from Heavitree stone.

Lamp post detail
A quayside lamp post bears
the distinctive three towers which
appear on Exeter's Coat of Arms.